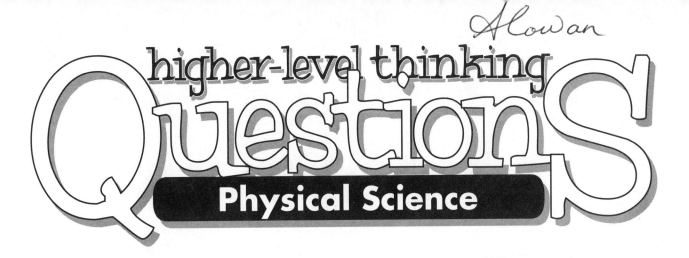

higher-level thinking Questions

Physical Science

D1360795

questions by
Miguel Kagan
Christa Chapman

created and designed by
Miguel Kagan

illustrated by
Celso Rodriguez

Kagan

Kagan

1160 Calle Cordillera

San Clemente, CA 92673

(949) 369-6310

Fax: (949) 369-6311

1 (800) WEE CO-OP

www.KaganOnline.com

ISBN: 1-879097-52-4

Table of Contents

"I had six
honest serving men
They taught me all I knew:
Their names were Where
and What and When
and Why and How and
Who.

— Rudyard Kipling

Introduction

In your hands you hold a powerful book. It is a member of a series of transformative blackline activity books. Between the covers, you will find questions, questions, and more questions! But these are no ordinary questions. These are the important kind—higher-level thinking questions—the kind that stretch your students' minds; the kind that release your students' natural curiosity about the world; the kind that rack your students' brains; the kind that instill in your students a sense of wonderment about your curriculum.

But we are getting a bit ahead of ourselves. Let's start from the beginning. Since this is a book of questions, it seems only appropriate for this introduction to pose a few questions—about the book and its underlying educational philosophy. So Mr. Kipling's Six Honest Serving Men, if you will, please lead the way:

What?
What are higher-level thinking questions?

This is a loaded question (as should be all good questions). Using our analytic thinking skills, let's break this question down into two smaller questions: 1) What is higher-level thinking? and 2) What are questions? When we understand the types of thinking skills and the types of questions, we can combine the best of both worlds, crafting beautiful questions to generate the range of higher-level thinking in our students!

Types of Thinking

There are many different types of thinking. Some types of thinking include:

- applying
- associating
- comparing
- contrasting
- defining
- elaborating
- empathizing
- experimenting
- generalizing
- investigating
- making analogies
- planning
- prioritizing
- recalling
- reflecting
- reversing
- sequencing
- summarizing
- synthesizing
- assessing
- augmenting
- connecting
- decision-making
- drawing conclusions
- eliminating
- evaluating
- explaining
- inferring consequences
- inventing
- memorizing
- predicting
- problem-solving
- reducing
- relating
- role-taking
- substituting
- symbolizing
- understanding
- thinking about thinking (metacognition)

This is quite a formidable list. It's nowhere near complete. Thinking is a big, multifaceted phenomenon. Perhaps the most widely recognized system for classifying thinking and classroom questions is Benjamin Bloom's Taxonomy of Thinking Skills. Bloom's Taxonomy classifies thinking skills into six hierarchical levels. It begins with the lower levels of thinking skills and moves up to higher-level thinking skills: 1) Knowledge, 2) Comprehension, 3) Application, 4) Analysis, 5) Synthesis, 6) Evaluation. See Bloom's Taxonomy on the following page.

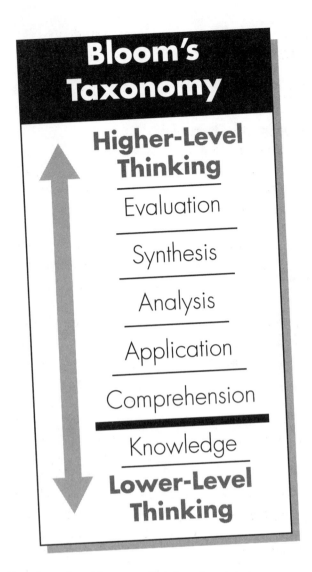

Bloom's Taxonomy

Higher-Level Thinking

Evaluation

Synthesis

Analysis

Application

Comprehension

Knowledge

Lower-Level Thinking

In education, the term "higher-level thinking" often refers to the higher levels of Mr. Bloom's taxonomy. But Bloom's Taxonomy is but one way of organizing and conceptualizing the various types of thinking skills.

There are many ways we can cut the thinking skills pie. We can alternatively view the many different types of thinking skills as, well…many different skills. Some thinking skills may be hierarchical. Some may be interrelated. And some may be relatively independent.

In this book, we take a pragmatic, functional approach. Each type of thinking skill serves a different function. So called "lower-level" think-ing skills are very useful for certain purposes. Memorizing and understanding information are

invaluable skills that our students will use throughout their lives. But so too are many of the "higher-level" thinking skills on our list. The more facets of students' thinking skills we develop, the better we prepare them for lifelong success.

Because so much classroom learning heretofore has focused on the "lower rungs" of the thinking skills ladder—knowledge and comprehension, or memorization and understanding—in this series of books we have chosen to focus on questions to generate "higher-level" thinking. This book is an attempt to correct the imbalance in the types of thinking skills developed by classroom questions.

Types of Questions

As we ask questions of our students, we further promote cognitive development when we use Fat questions, Low-Consensus questions, and True questions.

Fat Questions vs. Skinny Questions

Skinny questions are questions that require a skinny answer. For example, after reading a poem, we can ask: "Did you like the poem?" Even though this question could be categorized as an Evaluation question—Bloom's highest level of thinking— it can be answered with one monosyllabic word: "Yes" or "No." How much thinking are we actually generating in our students?

We can reframe this question to make it a fat question: "What things did you like about the poem? What things did you dislike?" Notice no short answer will do. Answering this fattened-up question requires more elaboration. These fat questions presuppose not that there is only one thing but things plural that the student liked and things that she did not like. Making things plural is one way to make skinny questions fat. Stu-dents stretch their minds to come up with multiple ideas or solutions. Other easy ways to

Higher-Level Thinking Questions for Physical Science
Kagan • 1 (800) WEE CO-OP • www.KaganOnline.com

make questions fat is to add "Why or why not?" or "Explain" or "Describe" or "Defend your position" to the end of a question. These additions promote elaboration beyond a skinny answer. Because language and thought are intimately intertwined, questions that require elaborate responses stretch students' thinking: They grapple to articulate their thoughts.

The type of questions we ask impact not just the type of thinking we develop in our students, but also the depth of thought. Fat questions elicit fat responses. Fat responses develop both depth of thinking and range of thinking skills. The questions in this book are designed to elicit fat responses—deep and varied thinking.

High-Consensus Questions vs. Low-Consensus Questions

A high-consensus question is one to which most people would give the same response, usually a right or wrong answer. After learning about sound, we can ask our students: "What is the name of a room specially designed to improve acoustics for the audience?" This is a high-consensus question. The answer (auditorium) is either correct or incorrect.

Compare the previous question with a low-consensus question: "If you were going to build an auditorium, what special design features would you take into consideration?" Notice, to the low-consensus question there is no right or wrong answer. Each person formulates his or her unique response. To answer, students must apply what they learned, use their ingenuity and creativity.

High-consensus questions promote convergent thinking. With high-consensus questions we strive to direct students **what to think**. Low-consensus questions promote divergent thinking, both critical and creative. With low-consen-

sus questions we strive to develop students' **ability to think**. The questions in this book are low-consensus questions designed to promote independent, critical and creative thought.

True Questions vs. Review Questions

We all know what review questions are. They're the ones in the back of every chapter and unit. Review questions ask students to regurgitate previously stated or learned information. For example, after learning about the rain forest we may ask: "What percent of the world's oxygen does the rain forest produce?" Students can go back a few pages in their books or into their memory banks and pull out the answer. This is great if we are working on memorization skills, but does little to develop "higher-order" thinking skills.

True questions, on the other hand, are meaningful questions—questions to which we do not know the answer. For example: "What might happen if all the world's rain forests were cut down?" This is a hypothetical; we don't know the answer but considering the question forces us to think. We infer some logical consequences based on what we know. The goal of true questions is not a correct answer, but the thinking journey students take to create a meaningful response. True questions are more representative of real life. Seldom is there a black and white answer. In life, we struggle with ambiguity, confounding variables, and uncertain outcomes. There are millions of shades of gray. True questions prepare students to deal with life's uncertainties.

When we ask a review question, we know the answer and are checking to see if the student does also. When we ask a true question, it is truly a question. We don't necessarily know the answer and neither does the student. True

> **Education is not the filling of a pail, but the lighting of a fire.**
> — William Butler Yeats

Types of Questions

Skinny ➤	Fat
• Short Answer	• Elaborated Answer
• Shallow Thinking	• Deep Thinking

High-Consensus ➤	Low-Consensus
• Right or Wrong Answer	• No Single Correct Answer
• Develops Convergent Thinking	• Develops Divergent Thinking
• "What" to Think	• "How" to Think

Review ➤	True
• Asker Knows Answer	• Asker Doesn't Know Answer
• Checking for Correctness	• Invitation to Think

questions are often an invitation to think, ponder, speculate, and engage in a questioning process.

We can use true questions in the classroom to make our curriculum more personally meaning-ful, to promote investigation, and awaken students' sense of awe and wonderment in what we teach. Many questions you will find in this book are true questions designed to make the content provocative, intriguing, and personally relevant.

The box above summarizes the different types of questions. The questions you will find in this book are a move away from skinny, high-consensus, review questions toward fat, low-consensus true questions. As we ask these types of questions in our class, we transform even mundane content into a springboard for higher-level thinking. As we integrate these question gems into our daily lessons, we create powerful learning experiences. ***We do not fill our students' pails with knowledge; we kindle their fires to become lifetime thinkers.***

 # Why?
Why should I use higher-level thinking questions in my classroom?

As we enter the new millennium, major shifts in our economic structure are changing the ways we work and live. The direction is increasingly toward an information-based, high-tech economy. The sum of our technological infor-mation is exploding. We could give you a figure how rapidly information is doubling, but by the time you read this, the number would be out-dated! No kidding.

But this is no surprise. This is our daily reality. We see it around us everyday and on the news: cloning, gene manipulation, e-mail, the Internet, Mars rovers, electric cars, hybrids, laser surgery, CD-ROMs, DVDs. All around us we see the wheels of progress turning: New discoveries, new technologies, a new societal knowledge and information base. New jobs are being created today in fields that simply didn't exist yesterday.

How do we best prepare our students for this uncertain future—a future in which the only constant will be change? As we are propelled into a world of ever-increasing change, what is the relative value of teaching students facts versus thinking skills? This point becomes even more salient when we realize that students cannot master everything, and many facts will soon become obsolete. Facts become outdated or irrelevant. Thinking skills are for a lifetime. Increasingly, how we define educational success will be away from the quantity of information mastered. Instead, we will define success as our students' ability to generate questions, apply, synthesize, predict, evaluate, compare, categorize.

If we as a professionals are to proactively respond to these societal shifts, thinking skills will become central to our curriculum. Whether we teach thinking skills directly, or we integrate them into our curriculum, the power to think is the greatest gift we can give our students!

We believe the questions you will find in this book are a step in the direction of preparing students for lifelong success. The goal is to develop independent thinkers who are critical and creative, regardless of the content. We hope the books in this series are more than sets of questions. We provide them as a model approach to questioning in the classroom.

On pages 8 and 9, you will find Questions to Engage Students' Thinking Skills. These pages contain numerous types of thinking and questions designed to engage each thinking skill. As you make your own questions for your students with your own content, use these question starters to help you frame your

> **Virtually the only predictable trend is continuing change.**
>
> — Dr. Linda Tsantis,
> Creating the Future

questions to stimulate various facets of your students' thinking skills. Also let your students use these question starters to generate their own higher-level thinking questions about the curriculum.

Who?
Who is this book for?

This book is for you and your students, but mostly for your students. It is designed to help make your job easier. Inside you will find hundreds of ready-to-use reproducible questions. Sometimes in the press for time we opt for what is easy over what is best. These books attempt to make easy what is best. In this treasure chest, you will find hours and hours of timesaving ready-made questions and activities.

Place Higher-Level Thinking In Your Students' Hands

As previously mentioned, this book is even more for your students than for you. As teachers, we ask a tremendous number of questions. Primary teachers ask 3.5 to 6.5 questions per minute! Elementary teachers average 348 questions a day. How many questions would you predict our students ask? Researchers asked this question. What they found was shocking: Typical students ask approximately one question per month.* One question per month!

Although this study may not be representative of your classroom, it does suggest that in general, as teachers we are missing out on a very powerful force—student-generated questions. The capacity to answer higher-level thinking questions is a

---

* Myra & David Sadker, "Questioning Skills" in *Classroom Teaching Skills*, 2nd ed. Lexington, MA: D.C. Heath & Co., 1982.

Questions to Engage Students' Thinking Skills

Analyzing
• How could you break down…?
• What components…?
• What qualities/characteristics…?

Applying
• How is _____ an example of…?
• What practical applications…?
• What examples…?
• How could you use…?
• How does this apply to…?
• In your life, how would you apply…?

Assessing
• By what criteria would you assess…?
• What grade would you give…?
• How could you improve…?

Augmenting/Elaborating
• What ideas might you add to…?
• What more can you say about…?

Categorizing/Classifying/Organizing
• How might you classify…?
• If you were going to categorize…?

Comparing/Contrasting
• How would you compare…?
• What similarities…?
• What are the differences between…?
• How is _____ different…?

Connecting/Associating
• What do you already know about…?
• What connections can you make between…?
• What things do you think of when you think of…?

Decision-Making
• How would you decide…?
• If you had to choose between…?

Defining
• How would you define…?
• In your own words, what is…?

Describing/Summarizing
• How could you describe/summarize…?
• If you were a reporter, how would you describe…?

Determining Cause/Effect
• What is the cause of…?
• How does _____ effect _____?
• What impact might…?

Drawing Conclusions/ Inferring Consequences
• What conclusions can you draw from…?
• What would happen if…?
• What would have happened if…?
• If you changed _____, what might happen?

Eliminating
• What part of _____ might you eliminate?
• How could you get rid of…?

Evaluating
• What is your opinion about…?
• Do you prefer…?
• Would you rather…?
• What is your favorite…?
• Do you agree or disagree…?
• What are the positive and negative aspects of…?
• What are the advantages and disadvantages…?
• If you were a judge…?
• On a scale of 1 to 10, how would you rate…?
• What is the most important…?
• Is it better or worse…?

Explaining
• How can you explain…?
• What factors might explain…?

Higher-Level Thinking Questions for Physical Science
Kagan • 1 (800) WEE CO-OP • www.KaganOnline.com

Experimenting
• How could you test…?
• What experiment could you do to…?

Generalizing
• What general rule can…?
• What principle could you apply…?
• What can you say about all…?

Interpreting
• Why is ____ important?
• What is the significance of…?
• What role…?
• What is the moral of…?

Inventing
• What could you invent to…?
• What machine could…?

Investigating
• How could you find out more about…?
• If you wanted to know about…?

Making Analogies
• How is ____ like ____?
• What analogy can you invent for…?

Observing
• What observations did you make about…?
• What changes…?

Patterning
• What patterns can you find…?
• How would you describe the organization of…?

Planning
• What preparations would you…?

Predicting/Hypothesizing
• What would you predict…?
• What is your theory about…?
• If you were going to guess…?

Prioritizing
• What is more important…?
• How might you prioritize…?

Problem-Solving
• How would you approach the problem?
• What are some possible solutions to…?

Reducing/Simplifying
• In a word, how would you describe…?
• How can you simplify…?

Reflecting/Metacognition
• What would you think if…?
• How can you describe what you were thinking when…?

Relating
• How is ____ related to ____?
• What is the relationship between…?
• How does ____ depend on ____?

Reversing/Inversing
• What is the opposite of…?

Role-Taking/Empathizing
• If you were (someone/something else)…?
• How would you feel if…?

Sequencing
• How could you sequence…?
• What steps are involved in…?

Substituting
• What could have been used instead of…?
• What else could you use for…?
• What might you substitute for…?
• What is another way…?

Symbolizing
• How could you draw…?
• What symbol best represents…?

Synthesizing
• How could you combine…?
• What could you put together…?

wonderful skill we can give our students, as is the skill to solve problems. Arguably more important skills are the ability to find problems to solve and formulate questions to answer. If we look at the great thinkers of the world—the Einsteins, the Edisons, the Freuds—their thinking is marked by a yearning to solve tremendous questions and problems. It is this questioning process that distinguishes those who illuminate and create our world from those who merely accept it.

Make Learning an Interactive Process

Higher-level thinking is not just something that occurs between students' ears! Students benefit from an interactive process. This basic premise underlies the majority of activities you will find in this book.

As students discuss questions and listen to others, they are confronted with differing perspectives and are pushed to articulate their own thinking well beyond the level they could attain on their own. Students too have an enormous capacity to mediate each other's learning. When we heterogeneously group students to work together, we create an environment to move students through their zone of proximal development. We also provide opportunities for tutoring and leadership. Verbal interaction with peers in cooperative groups adds a dimension to questions not available with whole-class questions and answers.

> **Asking a good question requires students to think harder than giving a good answer.**
> — Robert Fisher, Teaching Children to Learn

Reflect on this analogy: If we wanted to teach our students to catch and throw, we could bring in one tennis ball and take turns throwing it to each student and having them throw it back to us. Alternatively, we could bring in twenty balls and have our students form small groups and have them toss the ball back and forth to each other. Picture the two classrooms: One with twenty balls being caught at any one moment, and the other with just one. In which class would students better and more quickly learn to catch and throw?

The same is true with thinking skills. When we make our students more active participants in the learning process, they are given dramatically more opportunities to produce their own thought and to strengthen their own thinking skills. Would you rather have one question being asked and answered at any one moment in your class, or twenty? Small groups mean more questioning and more thinking. Instead of rarely answering a teacher question or rarely generating their own question, asking and answering questions becomes a regular part of your students' day. It is through cooperative interaction that we truly turn our classroom into a higher-level think tank. The associated personal and social benefits are invaluable.

When?
When do I use higher-level thinking questions?

Do I use these questions at the beginning of the lesson, during the lesson, or after? The answer, of course, is all of the above.

Use these questions or your own thinking questions at the beginning of the lesson to provide a motivational set for the lesson. Pique students' interest about the content with some provocative questions: "What would happen if we didn't have gravity?" "Why did Pilgrims get along with some Native Americans, but not others?" "What do you think this book will be about?" Make the content personally relevant by bringing in students' own knowledge, experiences, and feelings about the content: "What do you know about spiders?" "What things do you like about mystery stories?" "How would you feel if explorers invaded your land and killed your family?" "What do you wonder about electricity?"

Use the higher-level thinking questions throughout your lessons. Use the many questions and activities in this book not as a replacement of your curriculum, but as an additional avenue to explore the content and stretch students' thinking skills.

Use the questions after your lesson. Use the higher-level thinking questions, a journal writing activity, or the question starters as an extension activity to your lesson or unit.

Or just use the questions as stand-alone sponge activities for students or teams who have finished their work and need a challenging project to work on.

It doesn't matter when you use them, just use them frequently. As questioning becomes a habitual part of the classroom day, students' fear of asking silly questions is diminished. As the ancient Chinese proverb states, "Those who ask a silly question may seem a fool for five minutes, but those who do not ask remain a fool for life."

The important thing is to never stop questioning.
— Albert Einstein

As teachers, we should make a conscious effort to ensure that a portion of the many questions we ask on a daily basis are those that move our students beyond rote memorization. When we integrate higher-level thinking questions into our daily lessons, we transform our role from transmitters of knowledge to engineers of learning.

Where?
Where should I keep this book?

Keep it close by. Inside there are 16 sets of questions. Pull it out any time you teach these topics or need a quick, easy, fun activity or journal writing topic.

How?
How do I get the most out of this book?

In this book you will find 16 topics arranged alphabetically. For each topic there are reproducible pages for: 1) 16 Question Cards, 2) a Journal Writing activity page, 3) and a Question Starters activity page.

1. Question Cards

The Question Cards are truly the heart of this book. There are numerous ways the Question Cards can be used. After the other activity pages are introduced, you will find a description of a variety of engaging formats to use the Question Cards.

Specific and General Questions

Some of the questions provided in this book series are content-specific and others are content-free. For example, the literature questions in the Literature books are content-specific. Questions for the Great Kapok Tree deal specifically with that literature selection. Some language arts questions in the Language Arts book, on the other hand, are content-free. They are general questions that can be used over and over again with new content. For example, the Book Review questions can be used after reading any book. The Story Structure questions can be used after reading any story. You can tell by glancing at the title of the set and some of the questions whether the set is content-specific or content-free.

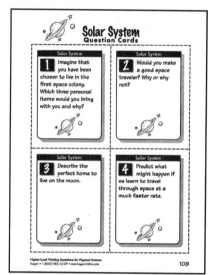

A Little Disclaimer

Not all of the "questions" on the Question Cards are actually questions. Some instruct students to do something. For example, "Compare and contrast…" We can also use these directives to develop the various facets of students' thinking skills.

The Power of Think Time

As you and your students use these questions, don't forget about the power of Think Time! There are two different think times. The first is the time between the question and the response. The second is the time between the response and feedback on the response. Think time has been shown to greatly enhance the quality of student thinking. If students are not pausing for either think time, or doing it too briefly, emphasize its importance. Five little seconds of silent think time after the question and five more seconds before feedback are proven, powerful ways to promote higher-level thinking in your class.

Use Your Question Cards for Years

For attractive Question Cards that will last for years, photocopy them on color card-stock paper and laminate them. To save time, have the Materials Monitor from each team pick up one card set, a pair of scissors for the team, and an envelope or rubber band. Each team cuts out their own set of Question Cards. When they are done with the activity, students can place the Question Cards in the envelope and write the name of the set on the envelope or wrap the cards with a rubber band for storage.

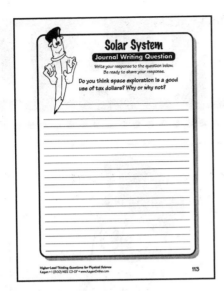

2. Journal Question

The Journal Writing page contains one of the 16 questions as a journal writing prompt. You can substitute any question, or use one of your own. The power of journal writing cannot be overstated. The act of writing takes longer than speaking and thinking. It allows the brain time to make deep connections to the content. Writing requires the writer to present his or her response in a clear, concise language. Writing develops both strong thinking and communication skills.

A helpful activity before journal writing is to have students discuss the question in pairs or in small teams. Students discuss their ideas and what they plan to write. This little prewriting activity ignites ideas for those students who stare blankly at their Journal Writing page. The interpersonal interaction further helps students articulate what they are thinking about the topic and invites students to delve deeper into the topic.

Tell students before they write that they will share their journal entries with a partner or with their team. This motivates many students to improve their entry. Sharing written responses also promotes flexible thinking with open-ended questions, and allows students to hear their peers' responses, ideas and writing styles.

Have students keep a collection of their journal entries in a three-ring binder. This way you can collect them if you wish for assessment or have students go back to reflect on their own learning. If you are using questions across the curriculum, each subject can have its own journal or own section within the binder. Use the provided blackline on the following page for a cover for students' journals or have students design their own.

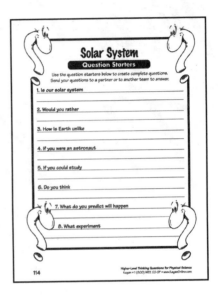

3. Question Starters

The Question Starters activity page is designed to put the questions in the hands of your students. Use these question starters to scaffold your students' ability to write their own thinking questions. This page includes eight question starters to direct students to generate questions across the levels and types of thinking. This Question Starters activity page can be used in a few different ways:

Individual Questions

Have students independently come up with their own questions. When done, they can trade their questions with a partner. On a separate sheet of paper students answer their partners' questions. After answering, partners can share how they answered each other's questions.

JOURNAL

My Best Thinking

_____

This Journal Belongs to

Pair Questions

Students work in pairs to generate questions to send to another pair. Partners take turns writing each question and also take turns recording each answer. After answering, pairs pair up to share how they answered each other's questions.

Team Questions

Students work in teams to generate questions to send to another team. Teammates take turns writing each question and recording each answer. After answering, teams pair up to share how they answered each other's questions.

Teacher-Led Questions

For young students, lead the whole class in coming up with good higher-level thinking questions.

Teach Your Students About Thinking and Questions

An effective tool to improve students' thinking skills is to teach students about the types of thinking skills and types of questions. Teaching students about the types of thinking skills improves their metacognitive abilities. When students are aware of the types of thinking, they may more effectively plan, monitor, and evaluate their own thinking. When students understand the types of questions and the basics of question construction, they are more likely to create effective higher-level thinking questions. In doing so they develop their own thinking skills and the thinking of classmates as they work to answer each other's questions.

Table of Activities

The Question Cards can be used in a variety of game-like formats to forge students' thinking skills. They can be used for cooperative team and pair work, for whole-class questioning, for independent activities, or at learning centers. On the following pages you will find numerous excellent options to use your Question Cards. As you use the Question Cards in this book, try the different activities listed below to add novelty and variety to the higher-level thinking process.

Activities

team activity #1

Question Commander

Preferably in teams of four, students shuffle their Question Cards and place them in a stack, questions facing down, so that all teammates can easily reach the Question Cards. Give each team a Question Commander set of instructions (blackline provided on following page) to lead them through each question.

Student One becomes the Question Commander for the first question. The Question Commander reads the question aloud to the team, then asks the teammates to think about the question and how they would answer it. After the think time, the Question Commander selects a teammate to answer the question. The Question Commander can spin a spinner or roll a die to select who will answer. After the teammate gives the answer, Question Commander again calls for think time, this time asking the team to think about the answer. After the think time, the Question Commander leads a team discus-

sion in which any teammember can contribute his or her thoughts or ideas to the question, or give praise or reactions to the answer.

When the discussion is over, Student Two becomes the Question Commander for the next question.

Question Commander
Instruction Cards

Question Commander

1. Ask the Question:
Question Commander reads the question to the team.
2. Think Time: "Think of your best answer."
3. Answer the Question:
The Question Commander selects a teammate to answer the question.
4. Think Time: "Think about how you would answer differently or add to the answer."
5. Team Discussion: As a team, discuss other possible answers or reactions to the answer given.

Question Commander

1. Ask the Question:
Question Commander reads the question to the team.
2. Think Time: "Think of your best answer."
3. Answer the Question:
The Question Commander selects a teammate to answer the question.
4. Think Time: "Think about how you would answer differently or add to the answer."
5. Team Discussion: As a team, discuss other possible answers or reactions to the answer given.

Question Commander

1. Ask the Question:
Question Commander reads the question to the team.
2. Think Time: "Think of your best answer."
3. Answer the Question:
The Question Commander selects a teammate to answer the question.
4. Think Time: "Think about how you would answer differently or add to the answer."
5. Team Discussion: As a team, discuss other possible answers or reactions to the answer given.

Question Commander

1. Ask the Question:
Question Commander reads the question to the team.
2. Think Time: "Think of your best answer."
3. Answer the Question:
The Question Commander selects a teammate to answer the question.
4. Think Time: "Think about how you would answer differently or add to the answer."
5. Team Discussion: As a team, discuss other possible answers or reactions to the answer given.

Fan-N-Pick

In a team of four, Student One fans out the question cards, and says, "Pick a card, any card!" Student Two picks a card and reads the question out loud to teammates. After five seconds of think time, Student Three gives his or her answer. After another five seconds of think time, Student Four paraphrases, praises, or adds to the answer given. Students rotate roles for each new round.

Spin-N-Think™

Spin-N-Think spinners are available from Kagan to lead teams through the steps of higher-level thinking. Students spin the Spin-N-Think™ spinner to select a student at each stage of the questioning to: 1) ask the question, 2) answer the question, 3) paraphrase and praise the answer, 4) augment the answer, and 5) discuss the question or answer. The Spin-N-Think™ game makes higher-level thinking more fun, and holds students accountable because they are often called upon, but never know when their number will come up.

Three-Step Interview

After the question is read to the team, students pair up. The first step is an interview in which one student interviews the other about the question. In the second step, students remain with their partner but switch roles: The interviewer becomes the interviewee. In the third step, the pairs come back together and each student in turn presents to the team what their partner shared. Three-Step Interview is strong for individual accountability, active listening, and paraphrasing skills.

Team Discussion

Team Discussion is an easy and informal way of processing the questions: Students read a question and then throw it open for discussion. Team Discussion, however, does not ensure that there is individual accountability or equal participation.

Think-Pair-Square

One student reads a question out loud to teammates. Partners on the same side of the table then pair up to discuss the question and their answers. Then, all four students come together for an open discussion about the question.

Question-Write-RoundRobin

Students take turns asking the team the question. After each question is asked, each student writes his or her ideas on a piece of paper. After students have finished writing, in turn they share their ideas. This format creates strong individual accountability because each student is expected to develop and share an answer for every question.

Mix-Pair-Discuss

Each student gets a different Question Card. For 16 to 32 students, use two sets of questions. In this case, some students may have the same question which is OK. Students get out of their seats and mix around the classroom. They pair up with a partner. One partner reads his or her Question Card and the other answers. Then they switch roles. When done they trade cards and find a new partner. The process is repeated for a predetermined amount of time. The rule is students cannot pair up with the same partner twice. Students may get the same questions twice or more, but each time it is with a new partner. This strategy is a fun, energizing way to ask and answer questions.

Think-Pair-Share

Think-Pair-Share is teacher-directed. The teacher asks the question, then gives students think time. Students then pair up to share their thoughts about the question. After the pair discussion, one student is called on to share with the class what was shared in his or her pair. Think-Pair-Share does not provide as much active participation for students as Think-Pair-Square because only one student is called upon at a time, but is a nice way to do whole-class sharing.

Inside-Outside Circle

Each student gets a Question Card. Half of the students form a circle facing out. The other half forms a circle around the inside circle; each student in the outside circle faces one student in the inside circle. Students in the outside circle ask inside circle students a question. After the inside circle students answer the question, students switch roles questioning and answering. After both have asked and answered a question, they each praise theother's answers and then hold up a hand indicating they are finished. When most students have a hand up, have students trade cards with their partner and rotate to a new partner. To rotate, tell the outside circle to move to the left. This format is a lively and enjoyable way to ask questions and have students listen to the thinking of many classmates.

Question & Answer

This might sound familiar: Instead of giving students the Question Cards, the teacher asks the questions and calls on one student at a time to answer. This traditional format eliminates simultaneous, cooperative interaction, but may be good for introducing younger students to higher-level questions.

Numbered Heads Together

Students number off in their teams so that every student has a number. The teacher asks a question. Students put their "heads together" to discuss the question. The teacher then calls on a number and selects a student with that number to share what his or her team discussed.

RallyRobin

Each pair gets a set of Question Cards. Student A in the pair reads the question out loud to his or her partner. Student B answers. Partners take turns asking and answering each question.

Pair Discussion

Partners take turns asking the question. The pair then discusses the answer together. Unlike RallyRobin, students discuss the answer. Both students contribute to answering and to discussing each other's ideas.

Question-Write-Share-Discuss

One partner reads the Question Card out loud to his or her teammate. Both students write down their ideas. Partners take turns sharing what they wrote. Partners discuss how their ideas are similar and different.

Journal Writing

Students pick one Question Card and make a journal entry or use the question as the prompt for an essay or creative writing. Have students share their writing with a partner or in turn with teammates.

Independent Answers

Students each get their own set of Questions Cards. Pairs or teams can share a set of questions, or the questions can be written on the board or put on the overhead projector. Students work by themselves to answer the questions on a separate sheet of paper. When done, students can compare their answers with a partner, teammates, or the whole class.

Center Ideas

1. Question Card Center

At one center, have the Question Cards and a Spin-N-Think™ spinner, Question Commander instruction card, or Fan-N-Pick instructions. Students lead themselves through the thinking questions. For individual accountability, have each student record their own answer for each question.

2. Journal Writing Center

At a second center, have a Journal Writing activity page for each student. Students can discuss the question with others at their center, then write their own journal entry. After everyone is done writing, students share what they wrote with other students at their center.

3. Question Starters Center

At a third center, have a Question Starters page. Split the students at the center into two groups. Have both groups create thinking questions using the Question Starters activity page. When the groups are done writing their questions, they trade questions with the other group at their center. When done answering each other's questions, two groups pair up to compare their answers.

Astronomy

higher-level thinking questions

Nothing is more fundamental to solid educational development than a pure, uncontaminated curiosity.

— Burton White,

The First Three Years of Life

Astronomy
Question Cards

1 There are 88 constellations in the sky. Some of their names are Pegasus, Aries (ram), Taurus (bull), Orion (hunter), Crux (cross). How might they have been named? If you found a new constellation, what would you name it?

2 Why do you think people believed that the earth was the center of the universe?

3 How do you think people kept track of the seasons before there were any calendars?

4 In 1608 Hans Lippershey, a Dutch astronomer, invented the telescope. What impact did the telescope have on astronomy?

Astronomy

5 Why might astronomers often study the sky from observatories on mountain tops and telescopes in space?

Astronomy

6 If you were given the opportunity to go into space, would you go knowing the risks?

Astronomy

7 You are in charge of designing a space suit for astronauts to spend time outside of their spacecraft. What will your space suit look like? What materials will you use? What special features will it have?

Astronomy

8 How big is the universe? Explain your answer.

Higher-Level Thinking Questions for Physical Science
Kagan • 1 (800) WEE CO-OP • www.KaganOnline.com

Astronomy
Question Cards

Astronomy

9 We shouldn't waste time and money studying the stars when there are starving people in the world. Do you agree or disagree? Explain.

Astronomy

10 Not too long ago, travel to the moon was just a dream. Where do you predict space exploration will take humans in the next 50 years?

Astronomy

11 You work for NASA designing the first space shuttle. You know that on re-entry into Earth's atmosphere, parts of the shuttle reach 2,900 degrees Fahrenheit. How will you protect your astronauts from burning up?

Astronomy

12 You are in charge of designing a remote controlled vehicle that will collect information from a newly discovered planet. How will you operate your space probe? What will it do? What will it look like?

Astronomy

13 It is estimated that Earth was formed over 4 billion years ago. What will be different in another 4 billion years?

Astronomy

14 What would be different if it took Earth 1,000 days to completely orbit the sun instead of 365 days?

Astronomy

15 Would you want to be an astronomer? Why or why not?

Astronomy

16 How are astronomers like oceanographers? How are they different?

Astronomy

Journal Writing Question

Write your response to the question below.
Be ready to share your response.

You are in charge of designing a space suit for astronauts to spend time outside of their spacecraft. What will your space suit look like? What materials will you use? What special features will it have?

_____

_____

_____

_____

_____

_____

_____

_____

_____

_____

_____

_____

_____

_____

Astronomy

Question Starters

Use the question starters below to create complete questions.
Send your questions to a partner or to another team to answer.

1. If you were an astronomer

2. Do you think

3. What do you wonder

4. What do you predict

5. How is astronomy like

6. In your opinion, what is the most fascinating

7. What is the relationship

8. What advances

Higher-Level Thinking Questions for Physical Science
Kagan • 1 (800) WEE CO-OP • www.KaganOnline.com

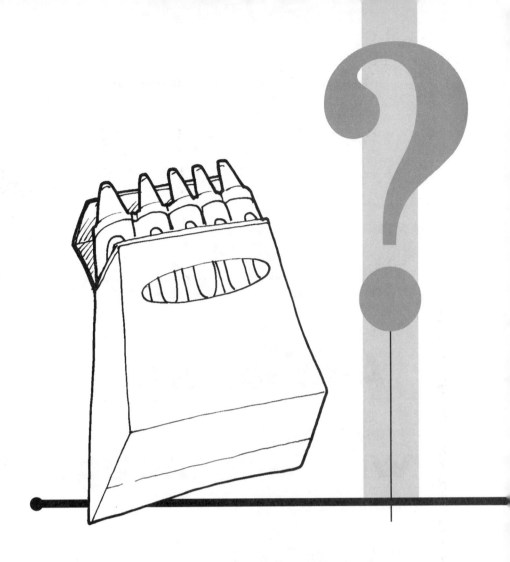

Color

higher-level thinking questions

"We are what we think. All that we are arises with our thoughts. With our thoughts, we make our world."

— Buddha

Color
Question Cards

Color

1 What is your favorite color? Why is it your favorite?

Color

2 What emotion does the color red best represent? How about blue? Green? Orange? Yellow?

Color

3 How many colors are there? Explain your answer.

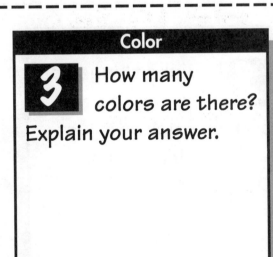

Color

4 How does an artist use color?

Color
Question Cards

5 Describe what the world would look like if you couldn't see colors.

6 What is the most colorful thing you've ever seen in your life? Describe it. What makes it so colorful?

7 Why do you think sports teams and companies have their own unique colors?

8 Some things you expect to be a certain color or it just wouldn't look right. Describe three examples.

Higher-Level Thinking Questions for Physical Science
Kagan • 1 (800) WEE CO-OP • www.KaganOnline.com

Color
Question Cards

9 Name three "cool" colors and three "warm" colors. Why do we call them cool and warm if colors don't have a temperature?

10 What color best describes your personality? Why?

11 Do you think black and white should be considered colors? How are they different from other colors?

12 How are color lights similar to color paints? How are they different?

Color
Question Cards

Color

13 If everything had to be one color, what color would you choose? Why?

Color

14 Some animals are very colorful (parrots) and others very plain (bears). What are the advantages and disadvantages of being colorful?

Color

15 How would you describe "green" to a blind person?

Color

16 Are you good at coordinating the colors you wear? If so, what's your secret? If not, why not?

Higher-Level Thinking Questions for Physical Science
Kagan • 1 (800) WEE CO-OP • www.KaganOnline.com

Color

Journal Writing Question

Write your response to the question below.
Be ready to share your response.

**What color best describes your personality?
Why?**

_____

_____

_____

_____

_____

_____

_____

_____

_____

_____

_____

_____

_____

_____

_____

_____

Color

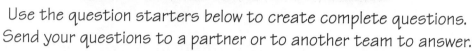
Question Starters

Use the question starters below to create complete questions.
Send your questions to a partner or to another team to answer.

1. How is color _____

_____

2. If there were no colors _____

_____

3. Why do we see _____

_____

4. What do you wonder about _____

_____

5. If you had to choose _____

_____

6. If you were an artist _____

_____

7. What is _____

_____

8. What role does color play _____

_____

Higher-Level Thinking Questions for Physical Science
Kagan • 1 (800) WEE CO-OP • www.KaganOnline.com

Electricity

higher-level thinking questions

"It is astonishing what an effort it seems to be for many people to put their brains definitely and systematically to work."

— Thomas Edison

Electricity
Question Cards

1 Nuclear plants generate electricity. But they would be extremely hazardous if they had a meltdown. Do you think we should use nuclear energy? Why or why not?

2 Was electricity invented or discovered? What's the difference between an invention and a discovery?

3 What would happen if a storm knocked out the electricity in your town, and it couldn't be restored for a month? Sequence the events that might occur.

4 Soon all cars, boats and airplanes will all run on electricity. Do you agree or disagree? Why?

Electricity
Question Cards

5 Mechanical energy can be converted into electrical energy and electrical energy can be converted into mechanical energy. What does this tell you about energy and electricity?

6 What do you know about electricity? What would you like to find out?

7 What are the dangers of electricity in your house?

8 Electricity is the greatest discovery of all time. Do you agree or disagree?

Higher-Level Thinking Questions for Physical Science
Kagan • 1 (800) WEE CO-OP • www.KaganOnline.com

Electricity
Question Cards

9 Creating electricity requires money, time and resources. How can you conserve electricity?

10 What inventions did electricity make possible?

11 When you plug a plug into an outlet, you have electricity. How does electricity get to your house?

12 Do you think being an electrician would be a good job for you? Why or why not?

Electricity
Question Cards

13 How was the world different before people had electricity in their houses?

14 List five electrical appliances you have in your house? Rank them from 1 to 5 in importance.

15 How could you test to see if something conducts electricity? How could you test to see what conducts electricity better?

16 What is the difference between a battery and an outlet? How are they similar?

Higher-Level Thinking Questions for Physical Science
Kagan • 1 (800) WEE CO-OP • www.KaganOnline.com

Electricity

Journal Writing Question

Write your response to the question below.
Be ready to share your response.

What would happen if a storm knocked out the electricity in your town, and it couldn't be restored for a month? Sequence the events that might occur.

_____
_____
_____
_____
_____
_____
_____
_____
_____
_____
_____
_____
_____
_____
_____
_____
_____
_____

Electricity

Question Starters

Use the question starters below to create complete questions.
Send your questions to a partner or to another team to answer.

1. Is electricity

2. What things depend

3. In the future

4. What do you know about

5. What dangers

6. What would be different if

7. How is electricity like

8. How could you test

Higher-Level Thinking Questions for Physical Science
Kagan • 1 (800) WEE CO-OP • www.KaganOnline.com

Force and
Motion

higher-level thinking questions

"The highest function of the teacher consists not so much in imparting knowledge as in stimulating the pupil in its love and pursuit.

— Henri Frederic Amiel

 # Force and Motion
Question Cards

Force and Motion

1 What would happen if you played tug of war on ice? There is less friction on the ice. Explain.

Force and Motion

2 What might explain why a feather and a rock fall to the ground together on the moon, but not on Earth?

Force and Motion

3 If the earth is always rotating, why doesn't it feel like we're spinning?

Force and Motion

4 Which would be easier to push, a bus or a car? Why? Which would be harder to stop? Why? Make a general statement or formulate a principle based on this example.

5 What does the shape of a car have to do with its speed and gas mileage?

6 Motion is relative. If you are standing still, and someone rides by on a skateboard, he is not the only one moving. Explain why.

7 Due to gravity, ocean tides are highest (spring tides) when the moon and sun are on the same side of Earth. How could you find out if the sun or moon's gravity had more influence on the tide?

8 Newton's third law of motion states, "To every action there is an equal and opposite reaction." Give an example of this law from your everyday experience.

Higher-Level Thinking Questions for Physical Science
Kagan • 1 (800) WEE CO-OP • www.KaganOnline.com

Force and Motion

9 Lubricants (oil and grease) reduce friction and heat by allowing objects to slide past each other more easily. Where have you seen a lubricant used? What was it used for?

Force and Motion

10 Air has weight. Air near Earth is pressed down by the air above. At higher elevations, the pressure decreases. Use this information to explain why we often have to clear our ears when we fly or when we drive to the mountains.

Force and Motion

11 Centrifugal force pushes outward. Centripetal force pulls inward. Give an example of these two forces in action.

Force and Motion

12 A perpetual motion machine is supposed to run by itself forever. Why do you think people have been unsuccessful in inventing one?

Force and Motion
Question Cards

13 If you drop a tennis ball out of your car window while driving, what do you think the tennis ball will do? Why? What experiment could you do at school to test your theory?

14 The principle of inertia states that every object remains stopped or goes on moving at a steady rate in a straight line unless acted upon by another force. Give an example of this principle.

15 What would happen here on Earth if the Sun's gravitational pull was stronger than Earth's?

16 As a pilot accelerates in a jet or spacecraft, he or she feels much heavier than normal. Why might this happen?

56

Higher-Level Thinking Questions for Physical Science
Kagan • 1 (800) WEE CO-OP • www.KaganOnline.com

Force and Motion
Journal Writing Question

Write your response to the question below.
Be ready to share your response.

What would happen if things fell up instead of down?

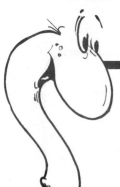

Force and Motion
Question Starters

Use the question starters below to create complete questions.
Send your questions to a partner or to another team to answer.

1. What forces

2. How could you test

3. What might happen if

4. What principle

5. How is motion

6. Where might

7. If you wanted to

8. What do you wonder about

Higher-Level Thinking Questions for Physical Science
Kagan • 1 (800) WEE CO-OP • www.KaganOnline.com

Gravity

higher-level thinking questions

"Learning is not just knowing the answers."

— Charles Handy,
The Age of Unreason

Gravity
Question Cards

Gravity

1 If we can't see, hear, touch, taste, or smell gravity, how do we know it exists?

Gravity

2 What would happen if gravity pulled things down at a different rate each day?

Gravity

3 What do you think falls faster, a marble or a bowling ball? How could you test to see if you're right?

Gravity

4 Jupiter is the biggest planet in our solar system. Its mass is 318 times greater than Earth's mass. If you could walk on Jupiter, what would it feel like?

Gravity
Question Cards

Gravity
Question Cards

Gravity

9 You invented an antigravity machine. Who will you try to sell it to? Why?

Gravity

10 You meet an alien who lives in outer space. He doesn't know what gravity is. How could you explain it to him?

Gravity

11 If you stood on a scale in an elevator and went up or down, would your weight register differently on the scale? Why or why not?

Gravity

12 Why is it easy to ride your bike downhill, but difficult to ride uphill. Explain.

Gravity
Question Cards

Gravity

13 In what ways do people use gravity to make work easier? Name three uses of gravity.

Gravity

14 Your brother jumps off a low diving board. Your sister jumps off the high dive. Your sister is going faster when she hits the water? Why?

Gravity

15 How does a balance use gravity to compare weights?

Gravity

16 If you knew that on Saturday there would be no more gravity, what preparations would you make?

Gravity
Journal Writing Question

Write your response to the question below.
Be ready to share your response.

If you knew that on Saturday there would be no more gravity, what preparations would you make?

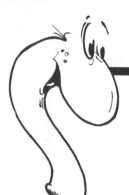

Gravity
Question Starters

Use the question starters below to create complete questions.
Send your questions to a partner or to another team to answer.

1. On the sun

2. What might happen if

3. How could you represent

4. If there was no gravity

5. What plans would you make if

6. How can you explain

7. How is gravity like

8. What depends on

Higher-Level Thinking Questions for Physical Science
Kagan • 1 (800) WEE CO-OP • www.KaganOnline.com

Heat

higher-level thinking questions

"All the resources we need are in the mind.

— Theodore Roosevelt

Heat
Question Cards

Heat

1 Does water keep getting hotter and hotter the longer it boils? How could you test to see if it does?

Heat

2 If you are cold, what are some things you can do to warm up? List three ideas and describe how each works to heat you up.

Heat

3 Why do you think there are three main temperature scales (Fahrenheit, Celsius, and Kelvin) instead of just one?

Heat

4 What is heat? Where does it come from?

Heat
Question Cards

Heat

5 What would absorb more heat: a mirror, white cement, or black asphalt? What experiment could you do to test to see if you were right?

Heat

6 What are some appliances in your house that generate heat? List five. How could you sort them into categories?

Heat

7 What are some dangers associated with heat?

Heat

8 How does a thermometer work to measure how hot something is? What are some uses for a thermometer?

Higher-Level Thinking Questions for Physical Science
Kagan • 1 (800) WEE CO-OP • www.KaganOnline.com

Heat
Question Cards

Heat

9 Insulation keeps heat in houses when it's cold outside and keeps the heat out when it's hot outside. How does insulation work?

Heat

10 What is the hottest thing you can think of? What makes it so hot? What is the coldest thing you can think of? What makes it so cold?

Heat

11 When you turn on the hot water faucet in your house, you get hot water. How does it get hot? Trace the sequence of steps to get hot water.

Heat

12 How could you test to see if hot air really does rise?

Heat
Question Cards

Heat

13 Hot and cold refer to temperature. How else do we use the words "Hot" and "Cool?"

Heat

14 Would you rather be too hot or too cold? Why?

Heat

15 Why do you think some places on Earth are hot all year while others don't even get hot for a day?

Heat

16 When you put a spoon in a bowl of hot soup, the spoon will heat up. This is called conduction. Metal is a good conductor of heat. What are some other good conductors? What are some bad conductors?

Higher-Level Thinking Questions for Physical Science
Kagan • 1 (800) WEE CO-OP • www.KaganOnline.com

Heat

Journal Writing Question

Write your response to the question below.
Be ready to share your response.

How could you test to see if hot air really does rise?

_____
_____
_____
_____
_____
_____
_____
_____
_____
_____
_____
_____
_____
_____
_____
_____
_____

Heat

Question Starters

Use the question starters below to create complete questions.
Send your questions to a partner or to another team to answer.

1. In your life

2. What things

3. What general rule

4. Is heat

5. What is the relationship between

6. Why do you think heat

7. How do scientists

8. What might happen if

Higher-Level Thinking Questions for Physical Science
Kagan • 1 (800) WEE CO-OP • www.KaganOnline.com

Investigating
Invention

higher-level thinking questions

"There is no expedient to which a man will not go to avoid the real labor of thinking."

— Thomas Edison

Investigating Invention
Question Cards

Investigating Invention

1 Predict what might be the next technological invention.

Investigating Invention

2 How would your life be different without the invention of keeping track of time?

Investigating Invention

3 Do you consider a new recipe to be an invention? Why or why not?

Investigating Invention

4 Choose an inventor you appreciate and explain why.

Investigating Invention
Question Cards

Investigating Invention

5 What could you invent to make your life easier?

Investigating Invention

6 Choose a recent invention and evaluate its usefulness.

Investigating Invention

7 Choose one invention in your home and explain how life would be different without it.

Investigating Invention

8 How has the invention of the personal computer affected society?

Higher-Level Thinking Questions for Physical Science
Kagan • 1 (800) WEE CO-OP • www.KaganOnline.com

Investigating Invention
Question Cards

Investigating Invention

9 Imagine life before the invention of the car. Was it better or worse? Why?

Investigating Invention

10 Do you think the invention of nuclear energy was a positive contribution to the world? Why or why not?

Investigating Invention

11 In your opinion, which invention has caused the most damage to society? Why?

Investigating Invention

12 Name an invention created in the 1800s that is still effective today. Which invention created in the 1900s will probably still be effective 1,000 years from now?

Investigating Invention
Question Cards

Investigating Invention

13 Invention comes from need. What need does your class have now? What could you invent to meet that need?

Investigating Invention

14 What characteristics might make a *good* inventor?

Investigating Invention

15 The telephone has come a long way since the first phone conversation. How might electronic communication be different in 100 years?

Investigating Invention

16 What *do* you think was the single most important invention in history? Why?

Higher-Level Thinking Questions for Physical Science
Kagan • 1 (800) WEE CO-OP • www.KaganOnline.com

Investigating Invention

Journal Writing Question

Write your response to the question below.
Be ready to share your response.

How has the invention of the personal computer affected society?

_____

_____

_____

_____

_____

_____

_____

_____

_____

_____

_____

_____

_____

_____

_____

_____

_____

_____

_____

Investigating Invention
Question Starters

Use the question starters below to create complete questions.
Send your questions to a partner or to another team to answer.

1. Which inventor

2. If you were an inventor

3. Do you think a patent

4. What impact

5. Do all inventions

6. How do inventors

7. Which invention

8. What is the most important

Higher-Level Thinking Questions for Physical Science
Kagan • 1 (800) WEE CO-OP • www.KaganOnline.com

Light

higher-level thinking questions

"Every clarification breeds new questions.

— Arthur Bloch

Light
Question Cards

Light

1 What would happen if the sun burned out and didn't produce any more light? Describe a sequence of events that might occur.

Light

2 What are some ways we humans have learned to make our own light? List five ideas. How could you categorize your ideas?

Light

3 Is a red apple still red when the lights are turned off, or does it only appear to be red because of the way its structure reflects light? Defend your position to someone who disagrees.

Light

4 How would the world be different if the sun did not set and it stayed light all the time?

Light
Question Cards

5 Light travels at the greatest possible velocity, about 186,000 miles per second. If you didn't know this, how could you measure how fast light travels? Describe your experiment.

6 What do you know about rainbows and why they appear?

7 How is a lantern like a spotlight? How is it different? Compare and contrast the two.

8 When light passes through a glass prism, it breaks into separate bands of different color. Why might this happen?

Higher-Level Thinking Questions for Physical Science
Kagan • 1 (800) WEE CO-OP • www.KaganOnline.com

Light
Question Cards

Light

9 Why do you think your shadow is shortest in the middle of the day? Can you ever have a shadow at night? Why or why not?

Light

10 What would happen if light slowed down to the pace of a snail?

Light

11 If you were going to write an article about light, what title would you use for your article to capture attention?

Light

12 If a star one light year away burned out today, would we still see its light tonight? Why or why not?

Light
Question Cards

Light

13 An object that reflects light of all wavelengths in equal amounts looks white. What color do you think an object that absorbs light of all wavelengths in equal amounts looks like? Explain the difference between light and dark things in sunlight.

Light

14 Some places in the world rarely get sunny days. How do you think this effects the people who live there?

Light

15 You have superpower sight. You can see in the dark. What will you do with your superpower?

Light

16 The spectrum of visible light from shortest to longest wavelength is Red, Orange, Yellow, Green, Blue, Indigo, Violet (ROY G. BIV). An object that absorbs shorter wavelengths of light but reflects longer wavelengths, looks red. Use this information to explain why a violet object looks violet.

Higher-Level Thinking Questions for Physical Science
Kagan • 1 (800) WEE CO-OP • www.KaganOnline.com

Light

Journal Writing Question

Write your response to the question below.
Be ready to share your response.

What would happen if the sun burned out
and didn't produce any more light? Describe
a sequence of events that might occur.

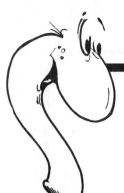

Light

Use the question starters below to create complete questions.
Send your questions to a partner or to another team to answer.

1. Why is light

2. What effects

3. Is the sun

4. If you wanted to test

5. How did electricity

6. What is the difference between

 7. What alternative

8. What role does light

Matter and Energy

higher-level thinking questions

"If everybody thought before they spoke, the silence would be deafening."

— George Barzan

Matter and Energy
Question Cards

Matter and Energy

1 Matter is made of tiny atoms. A speck of dust has a quadrillion atoms. What would happen if atoms were as big as marbles?

Matter and Energy

2 If you discovered a new element, what would you call it? Why?

Matter and Energy

3 If you were a scientist and figured out that splitting the atom could release a tremendous amount of energy, but that it could also be used to make an atomic bomb, would you share your amazing discovery?

Matter and Energy

4 Where does water go when it evaporates? Does it just disappear?

Matter and Energy
Question Cards

Matter and Energy

5 If you fill a glass bottle with water and stick it in the freezer, the bottle will probably break. Why?

Matter and Energy

6 Imagine you are a drop of water. Describe the stages (liquid, solid, gas) of your life in terms of the water cycle.

Matter and Energy

7 Rust is a chemical reaction. The oxygen in air or water takes electrons from the atoms in the metal. Where have you seen rust? What did it look like?

Matter and Energy

8 The law of conservation of energy says that energy is never created or destroyed. Energy changes its state from one form to another. Give an example of this law.

Higher-Level Thinking Questions for Physical Science
Kagan • 1 (800) WEE CO-OP • www.KaganOnline.com

Matter and Energy
Question Cards

Matter and Energy

9 Fossil fuels (coal, oil, and gas) will eventually run out. Why are they called "fossil" fuels? What will we do when they run out?

Matter and Energy

10 How can we harness the energy of wind and water? What other natural forces we can use to generate energy?

Matter and Energy

11 When you put a spoon of sugar in water and stir, the sugar disappears. Where does it go? Can you get it back?

Matter and Energy

12 How are liquids, gases and solids similar? How are they different?

Matter and Energy
Question Cards

13 How is lightning created? Where does it go?

14 What would the world be like if there were no such things as solids, only liquids and gases?

15 Imagine if water flowed uphill, instead of downhill. What would happen if the flow of water reversed?

16 All living things on Earth depend on energy from the sun. Decribe how.

Higher-Level Thinking Questions for Physical Science
Kagan • 1 (800) WEE CO-OP • www.KaganOnline.com

Matter and Energy
Journal Writing Question

Write your response to the question below.
Be ready to share your response.

Matter is made of tiny atoms.
A speck of dust has a quadrillion atoms.
What would happen if atoms were as big as
marbles?

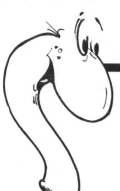

Matter and Energy
Question Starters

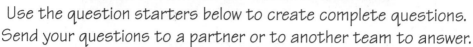

Use the question starters below to create complete questions.
Send your questions to a partner or to another team to answer.

1. Where is energy

2. If you wanted to test

3. What element

4. What do you wonder

5. What might happen if

6. What is the difference

7. How is matter

8. What could you invent to

Higher-Level Thinking Questions for Physical Science
Kagan • 1 (800) WEE CO-OP • www.KaganOnline.com

Simple Machines

higher-level thinking questions

"To find the exact answer, one must first ask the exact question.

— S. Tobin Webster

Simple Machines
Question Cards

Simple Machines

1 There are six types of simple machines:
1) Lever
2) Wheel and Axle
3) Inclined Plane
4) Screw
5) Wedge
6) Pulley
How have you seen each type used?

Simple Machines

2 Which type of simple machine do you think has had the most impact on modern inventions?

Simple Machines

3 A compound machine combines two or more simple machines. Name one compound machine and describe the simple machines involved.

Simple Machines

4 What do springs do? What have you seen them used for?

Simple Machines
Question Cards

Simple Machines

5 Besides transportation, where else have you seen a wheel and axle used? What did it do?

Simple Machines

6 You have:
1) 24 screws
2) a screwdriver
3) a saw
4) a sheet of plywood
5) a sheet of glass
6) a long wood board
What will you make? How will you make it?

Simple Machines

7 How does a door wedge work to keep a door open?

Simple Machines

8 How does an inclined plane or ramp make lifting easier? What impact does the slope of the ramp have on the work needed?

Higher-Level Thinking Questions for Physical Science
Kagan • 1 (800) WEE CO-OP • www.KaganOnline.com

Simple Machines
Question Cards

Simple Machines

9 Where have you seen ramps, and what were they used for?

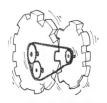

Simple Machines

10 How can gears change the speed or power of a machine? How can gears be used to alter the direction of movement? Give an example of each.

Simple Machines

11 If you were stranded on a deserted island and had a pulley, what could you use it for?

Simple Machines

12 Some machines harness Earth's natural energy. Give an example and describe how it works.

Simple Machines
Question Cards

13 The back of a hammer is a first-class lever that is used to pull out nails. Describe the effort, effort arm, fulcrum, load arm, and load in terms of a hammer pulling out a nail.

14 Complete the following sentence: "A machine is..."

15 Back in the Stone Age, using a lever may have meant moving a large rock with a stick. How might a lever be used today?

16 Which professions really need to understand how simple machines work? Why?

Higher-Level Thinking Questions for Physical Science
Kagan • 1 (800) WEE CO-OP • www.KaganOnline.com

Simple Machines
Journal Writing Question

Write your response to the question below.
Be ready to share your response.

There are six types of simple machines: 1) Lever, 2) Wheel and Axle, 3) Inclined Plane, 4) Screw, 5) Wedge, 6) Pulley. Describe how you've seen each one used.

_____

_____

_____

_____

_____

_____

_____

_____

_____

_____

_____

_____

_____

_____

_____

_____

_____

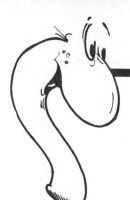

Simple Machines
Question Starters

Use the question starters below to create complete questions.
Send your questions to a partner or to another team to answer.

1. Where have you seen _____

2. How are gears _____

3. Why are wheels and axles _____

4. What simple machines _____

5. Why do pulleys _____

6. Is an inclined plane _____

7. What tool _____

8. Where might a wedge _____

Higher-Level Thinking Questions for Physical Science
Kagan • 1 (800) WEE CO-OP • www.KaganOnline.com

Solar System

higher-level thinking questions

"We do not know one millionth of one percent about anything.

— Thomas Edison

Solar System
Question Cards

Solar System

1 Imagine that you have been chosen to live in the first space colony. Which three personal items would you bring with you and why?

Solar System

2 Would you make a good space traveler? Why or why not?

Solar System

3 Describe the perfect home to live on the moon.

Solar System

4 Predict what might happen if we learn to travel through space at a much faster rate.

Solar System
Question Cards

Solar System

5 Do you think space exploration is a good use of tax dollars? Why or why not?

Solar System

6 Suppose the best movie of the year 2050 is filmed on Neptune. What do you think it will be about?

Solar System

7 Decide on which planet we may find life and tell why.

Solar System

8 Recently we have learned to create the perfect ball bearing, lightweight clothing, and long lasting nutritious food — all in space. What might be our next new "space product?"

Higher-Level Thinking Questions for Physical Science
Kagan • 1 (800) WEE CO-OP • www.KaganOnline.com

Solar System
Question Cards

9 Have you ever played Leap Frog? What does Leap Frog have to do with our use of space stations?

10 Think like a real estate salesperson. How would you market a home on Pluto to a potential customer?

11 What should be our next big space exploration?

12 You have just ordered a new dessert, "The Saturn," at your favorite restaurant. What will it look like and how will it taste?

Solar System
Question Cards

Solar System

13 Describe three important characteristics of an astronaut.

Solar System

14 Pretend you have landed on Venus. What might you see?

Solar System

15 Do you think humans will ever live on another planet? Why or why not?

Solar System

16 Who would you select for the crew of the first manned trip to Mars? Why?

Higher-Level Thinking Questions for Physical Science
Kagan • 1 (800) WEE CO-OP • www.KaganOnline.com

Solar System

Journal Writing Question

Write your response to the question below.
Be ready to share your response.

Do you think space exploration is a good use of tax dollars? Why or why not?

_____

_____

_____

_____

_____

_____

_____

_____

_____

_____

_____

_____

_____

_____

_____

_____

_____

_____

_____

Solar System

Question Starters

Use the question starters below to create complete questions.
Send your questions to a partner or to another team to answer.

1. Is our solar system

_____

2. Would you rather

_____

3. How is Earth unlike

_____

4. If you were an astronaut

_____

5. If you could study

_____

6. Do you think

_____

7. What do you predict will happen

_____

8. What experiment

_____

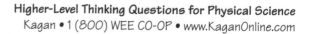

Higher-Level Thinking Questions for Physical Science
Kagan • 1 (800) WEE CO-OP • www.KaganOnline.com

Sound

higher-level thinking questions

"
You are today
where your thoughts
have brought you;
you will be tomorrow
where your thoughts
take you.
"

— James Allen

Higher-Level Thinking Questions for Physical Science
Kagan • 1 (800) WEE CO-OP • www.KaganOnline.com

Sound
Question Cards

Sound

1 What is your favorite sound? Why? What is your least favorite sound? Why?

Sound

2 If you could see sound it would look similar to the waves created by a pebble thrown in a pond. What would a shout look like? What would a whisper look like?

Sound

3 If a tree falls in a forest and no one is around to hear it, does it still make a sound? Why or why not?

Sound

4 When a jet goes faster than the speed of sound, we hear a sonic boom. Make a hypothesis about why we hear a sonic boom. How could you see if your hypothesis is correct?

Sound
Question Cards

Sound
5 If you were to sort the types of sounds we hear into categories, what categories would you create?

Sound
6 What are the ways people make sounds? Describe where the sounds come from.

Sound
7 What are some possible explanations for why deaf people can't hear?

Sound
8 If you could not see, how would you know where the sound was coming from?

Higher-Level Thinking Questions for Physical Science
Kagan • 1 (800) WEE CO-OP • www.KaganOnline.com

Sound
Question Cards

9 What are some things used to make sounds louder?

10 A doctor uses a stethoscope to listen to your heart or lungs. How does it work? What is similar to a stethoscope?

11 What is an echo? How do you think it is caused?

12 Auditoriums are rooms specially designed to improve the sounds for the audience. If you were going to design an auditorium, what special features would it have and why?

Sound
Question Cards

13 Bats send out high squeaking sounds and pick up the echoes to help them move around and find food. How might humans use SONAR (Sound Navigation And Ranging)?

14 Musical instruments make different sounds. Why do strings of a guitar or keys of a piano sound so different?

15 Can you think of an experiment to measure how fast sound travels?

16 Sound travels about 750 miles an hour. Light travels 186,416 miles in one second. What are some things you might see, but not hear until much later?

Sound

Write your response to the question below.
Be ready to share your response.

If a tree falls in a forest and no one is
around to hear it, does it still make a
sound? Why or why not?

_____
_____
_____
_____
_____
_____
_____
_____
_____
_____
_____
_____
_____
_____
_____
_____
_____
_____

Sound

Question Starters

Use the question starters below to create complete questions.
Send your questions to a partner or to another team to answer.

1. If you heard

2. Which sound

3. If you had supersonic hearing

4. What would happen if

5. Why are noises

6. If you couldn't hear

7. Why is sound

8. How does sound

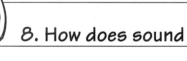

Higher-Level Thinking Questions for Physical Science
Kagan • 1 (800) WEE CO-OP • www.KaganOnline.com

Technology

higher-level thinking questions

"

Either you think — or else others have to think for you and take power from you, pervert and discipline your natural tastes, civilize and sterilize you.

"

— F. Scott Fitzgerald

Technology
Question Cards

1 What would happen if all the computers in the world shut down for the day?

2 How do you predict technology will change the world of the future?

3 When the Internet started, it was just a few computers linked together to share information. In what ways do you think the Internet will change in the future?

4 How do you use technology in your day-to-day life?

Technology
Question Cards

5 Technology is turning all of us into robots. Do you agree or disagree with this statement? Why or why not?

6 In the future, we will all have lots of free time because robots and computers will do our jobs for us. Do you agree or disagree?

7 Why do you think technology is scary for many people? Does it scare you? Why or why not?

8 Are there any disadvantages of technology? If not, why not? If so, what are they?

Higher-Level Thinking Questions for Physical Science
Kagan • 1 (800) WEE CO-OP • www.KaganOnline.com

Technology
Question Cards

Technology

9 Lots of things fit under the topic "technology." What categories could you use to organize the things you would consider technology?

Technology

10 If you could be involved in the development of one field of technology, what would it be? Explain.

Technology

11 Why do you think technological advances keep happening at an increasing rate?

Technology

12 If your best friend asked you, "What is technology?" how would you respond?

Technology
Question Cards

13 Some things that were science fiction in the past are actually happening today. Give an example. Do you think the science fiction of today will come true in the future? Give an example.

14 Should your education change as technology advances? If so, how should it change? If not, why not?

15 What do you think is humankind's greatest technological breakthrough?

16 How will human relations change as technology advances?

Higher-Level Thinking Questions for Physical Science
Kagan • 1 (800) WEE CO-OP • www.KaganOnline.com

Technology

Write your response to the question below.
Be ready to share your response.

When the Internet started, it was just a few computers linked together to share information. In what ways do you think the Internet will change in the future?

_____

_____

_____

_____

_____

_____

_____

_____

_____

_____

_____

_____

_____

_____

_____

_____

_____

_____

Technology
Question Starters

Use the question starters below to create complete questions.
Send your questions to a partner or to another team to answer.

1. What influence does technology

_____

_____

2. What are the disadvantages

_____

_____

3. What would be different if

_____

_____

4. What do you predict

_____

_____

5. What is the effect of

_____

_____

6. In the future

_____

_____

7. Will computers

_____

_____

8. If you were an inventor

_____

Higher-Level Thinking Questions for Physical Science
Kagan • 1 (800) WEE CO-OP • www.KaganOnline.com

Time

higher-level thinking questions

"Profundity of thought belongs to youth, clarity of thought to old age.

— Fredrich

Time
Question Cards

1 What is your favorite time of the day? Why is it your favorite time?

2 The time is different in different parts of the world. What would happen if it was the same time and same day everywhere?

3 When in your life did time seem to speed up, slow down or stand still?

4 Einstein said that we created time and ever since time has been controlling us. What did he mean?

Time
Question Cards

5 List five devices that keep track of time. Which ones do you use, and when do you use them?

6 There are 60 seconds in a minute, 60 minutes in an hour, 24 hours in a day, and 365 days in a year. Why might these numbers have been selected?

7 What happens to February 29th on leap year? Where does the day go?

8 What would happen if you woke up and all the clocks around the world stopped and wouldn't start again?

Time
Question Cards

Time

9 Complete the following simile: "Time is like..."

Time

10 What routines do you have in your day-to-day life based on the time of day?

Time

11 If you could freeze time for an hour for everyone, except for yourself, what would you do?

Time

12 Do you think time travel will ever be possible? Why or why not?

Time

13 If you could travel to the future, when and where would you go?

Time

14 How *do* clocks work to keep track of time?

Time

15 When did you have the, "Time of your life?"

Time

16 If you could travel into the past, what year would you go to? Where would you go?

Higher-Level Thinking Questions for Physical Science
Kagan • 1 (800) WEE CO-OP • www.KaganOnline.com

Time

Journal Writing Question

Write your response to the question below.
Be ready to share your response.

If you could travel to the future, when and where would you go?

_____
_____
_____
_____
_____
_____
_____
_____
_____
_____
_____
_____
_____
_____
_____
_____
_____
_____
_____
_____

Time

Question Starters

Use the question starters below to create complete questions.
Send your questions to a partner or to another team to answer.

1. What is the relationship

_____

2. Why is it important

_____

3. How does time

_____

4. What general rule

_____

5. If we had no clocks

_____

6. In your life

_____

 7. What song

_____

8. How is time like

_____

Higher-Level Thinking Questions for Physical Science
Kagan • 1 (800) WEE CO-OP • www.KaganOnline.com

Tools

higher-level thinking questions

Each thought is a nail that is driven

In structures that cannot decay;

And the mansion at last will be given

To us as we build it each day.

— George Eliot

Tools
Question Cards

Tools

1 If you were stranded on a deserted island and could only have one tool, which tool would you choose? What would you use it for?

Tools

2 The use of tools is what sets humans apart from other animals. Do you agree or disagree with this statement?

Tools

3 What do you think were the first tools humans used? What did they use them for?

Tools

4 What general statement can you make about all tools?

Tools
Question Cards

Tools

5 How many types of hammers can you name? Describe how each is used.

Tools

6 What has been more important to the progress of humankind: Tools or language? Explain why.

Tools

7 You have lots of different types of tools all over the place. You buy a new tool cabinet with eight drawers. How will you organize your cabinet?

Tools

8 What tool are you most like? Why?

Higher-Level Thinking Questions for Physical Science
Kagan • 1 (800) WEE CO-OP • www.KaganOnline.com

Tools
Question Cards

Tools

9 Learning how to use tools is much more important than learning history. Do you agree or disagree?

Tools

10 What have you made with a tool or tools that you are most proud of? What tool or tools did you use?

Tools

11 Invent a new tool. What will you call it? What will it be used for?

Tools

12 You want to build a birdhouse for your mom. What tools will you need? How will you use them?

Tools
Question Cards

Tools

13 The electric saw makes sawing quicker and easier than the handsaw. What other hand tools could be improved if they were electric? Describe how they would work.

Tools

14 What professions need to use a wrench? What do they use it for?

Tools

15 What tool is similar to a saw? How is it similar?

Tools

16 Would you rather be a toolmaker, tool inventor or tool user? Why?

Higher-Level Thinking Questions for Physical Science
Kagan • 1 (800) WEE CO-OP • www.KaganOnline.com

Tools

Write your response to the question below.
Be ready to share your response.

What have you made with a tool or tools that you are most proud of? What tool or tools did you use?

_____

_____

_____

_____

_____

_____

_____

_____

_____

_____

_____

_____

_____

_____

_____

_____

_____

_____

Tools

Question Starters

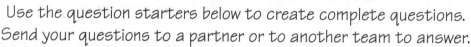

Use the question starters below to create complete questions.
Send your questions to a partner or to another team to answer.

1. How is a hammer _____

_____

2. What do we use _____

_____

3. If you were a carpenter _____

_____

4. If you wanted to build _____

_____

5. Who might _____

_____

6. What tools _____

_____

7. How could you categorize _____

_____

8. Why are tools _____

_____

Higher-Level Thinking Questions for Physical Science
Kagan • 1 (800) WEE CO-OP • www.KaganOnline.com

Transportation

higher-level thinking questions

"Thought is, perhaps, the forerunner and even the mother of ideas, and ideas are the most powerful and the most useful things in the world.

— George Gardner

Transportation
Question Cards

Transportation

1 What things do cars, boats, airplanes, buses, helicopters, motorcycles and bicycles all have in common?

Transportation

2 How would the world be different today if there were no airplanes?

Transportation

3 Should people give up their cars for more environmentally friendly mass transportation or is personal freedom more important than the environment?

Transportation

4 Transportation is continually evolving. What do you predict we will use for transportation in 100 years?

Transportation
Question Cards

Transportation

5 List the various types of transportation you have used in your life. When do you use each?

Transportation

6 How could we reduce or eliminate traffic? Why do you think your solution is not being used now?

Transportation

7 What are three disadvantages to modern transportation?

Transportation

8 At one time, the horse and carriage were a common form of transportation. Now it is almost obsolete (no longer used). Do you think the automobile will become obsolete?

Higher-Level Thinking Questions for Physical Science
Kagan • 1 (800) WEE CO-OP • www.KaganOnline.com

Transportation
Question Cards

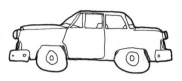

Transportation

9 If you were to design an alternative to the car and freeway, how would people get around?

Transportation

10 What will happen to transportation if fuel becomes scarce or runs out?

Transportation

11 Are there any traffic laws you don't agree with? Explain.

Transportation

12 What should be the legal driving age? Why? Should there be an age at which older people have their driving privileges taken away?

 # Transportation
Question Cards

Transportation

13 Do you prefer traveling by air, land or sea? Why?

Transportation

14 What role does transportation play in human relations?

Transportation

15 In what ways has transportation been improved to make the experience more enjoyable? What additional improvements would you suggest?

Transportation

16 Public safety is often an issue with transportation. What has been done to make travel safer? What else might be done?

Higher-Level Thinking Questions for Physical Science
Kagan • 1 (800) WEE CO-OP • www.KaganOnline.com

Transportation
Journal Writing Question

Write your response to the question below.
Be ready to share your response.

Transportation is continually evolving. What do you predict we will use for transportation in 100 years?

_____

_____

_____

_____

_____

_____

_____

_____

_____

_____

_____

_____

_____

_____

_____

_____

_____

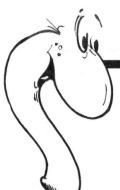

Transportation

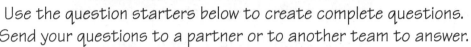

Question Starters

Use the question starters below to create complete questions.
Send your questions to a partner or to another team to answer.

1. If you had a car

_____

2. What effects

_____

3. Do you think motorcycles

_____

4. Would you rather

_____

5. Why is transportation

_____

6. Would a boat

_____

7. What if

_____

8. How are airplanes

_____

154